# THE IMMINENT CRISIS

---

**Greek Debt and the Collapse of the European Monetary Union**

---

Grant Wonders | Cambridge

ISBN 1-45286-633-3

EAN-13 978-1-45286-633-8

Printed in the United States of America by CreateSpace

Published in the United States of America
GW Publishing
383 Kirkland Mail Center
Cambridge, MA 02138

Cover design: Grant Wonders
Image: m_bartosch / FreeDigitalPhotos.net

# The Imminent Crisis V

"History makes clear that failure to achieve fiscal sustainability will, over time, sap the nation's economic vitality, reduce our living standards, and greatly increase the risk of economic and financial instability."

-Ben Bernanke, Chairman of the Board of Governors of the Federal Reserve

# THE IMMINENT CRISIS

---

Greek Debt and the Collapse of the European Monetary Union

---

Grant Wonders

# THE IMMINENT CRISIS

---

## Greek Debt and the Collapse of the European Monetary Union

---

Table of Contents

*Grant Wonders*
*May 2010*

# Author's Note

This book was inspired by my work in a Harvard Economics Department tutorial on the US and the World Economy. The focus of the class rested primarily on the US economic condition but dealt extensively with many relevant issues including our fiscal condition and mounting debt. With the Greek crisis, the most important distinction is the absence of a national currency. Although the benefits of the Euro to certain member states are undeniable, the analysis put forth here will demonstrate why the shared currency is ultimately unsustainable.

The first part of this book almost identically matches a paper that I wrote as part of my class and completed on March 7th, 2010. Despite the frozen temporality of the work and the inevitable lag between the time it was written and read, I believe it will prove to be a useful piece throughout the developing crisis and at its conclusion. Significantly, it captures the sentiment in early March when sovereign debt in certain Eurozone states stabilized after significant deterioration earlier in the year. Unlike most works that tend to be written ex-crisis, this book is written from an eye of the storm perspective. I hope that preserving the analysis in its original form, without the benefit of hindsight, will provide a unique insight for readers. The second part of the book transitions more broadly into the perils of global imbalance. It looks at the effects of excessive debt on the world economy and establishes a long-term roadmap for the eventual correction of imbalances. As a result of its broader scope, the analysis extends beyond the current crisis in the Eurozone. Instead, the focus rests increasingly on the United States as an engine for global economic growth.

Simultaneously, because this examination was purely academic in its inception, parts of it may seem a bit esoteric. Indeed, the first chapter in particular (on optimal currency area) may strain into an overly theoretical realm for the casual reader. However, it establishes an important framework for assessing the future, and admittedly much more exciting, chapters on the current crisis.

# PART ONE

*Grant Wonders*
*March 2010*

---

## The Eurozone

---

*Grant Wonders*
*March 2010*

# Prologue

The title of this work seems at first to be somewhat sensational. Many of the points that I have laid out here can be interpreted ambiguously if assessed only with theory. Indeed, I agree with much of the literature that has been written on the efficiencies of currency unions and the sustainability of the Euro, but throughout this book I have made every attempt to approach the developing crisis from a perspective of realism. The reality is that the unsustainable debt levels of Greece are fast developing into a full-blown crisis. Even more strikingly, they have exposed merely the tip of the iceberg in the specter that now hangs over Europe. The tension has reached a fever pitch and the socio-economic realities are fast guiding the inexorable collapse of the Euro.

# Assessing the Euro Currency Area

In building the framework for the startling implications of the current situation, it is perhaps helpful to take a step back and briefly reflect on the history of how we arrived at this juncture. The idea of a common currency shared by nations in Europe traces its origins to the work of Robert Mundell, a Nobel Laureate and Professor of Economics at Columbia, who is most recognized for his work on optimum currency areas.[1] A Theory of Optimum Currency Areas, published by Mundell in 1961, formed the theoretical foundations for the ideal region in which to share a currency. Applied broadly to a region such as Europe, the case has been made that the current members of the Eurozone meet many of the qualifications for optimized efficiency. Undeniably, the

---

[1] Mundell, R.A. (1961), "A Theory of Optimum Currency Areas", *American Economic Review*

European Union was largely convinced of these efficiencies when it set out the provisions for a currency union during the Masstricht Treaty of 1992.[2]

The most important prerequisite for a successful union is mobility. Capital needs to flow freely so that it can be allocated where it is most efficient. This necessarily, requires an integrated and open financial system that can transfer funds from those who wish to save towards those who will invest. Similarly, and perhaps much more problematically, labor must be mobile. Simultaneously, market efficiency demands that no binding constraints be imposed on economic participants that will distort participation. Factors here include flexible wages, rent rates, and pricing mechanisms that can adjust to meet the allocation demands of the market. The agreements of the Masstricht Treaty went a long way towards ensuring that the legal structure of the European Union would be conducive to free-markets as well as the unrestrained movements of labor and capital across international borders.

---

[2] Stauffer, Amity, "What is the European Monetary Union", *The University of Iowa Center for International Finance and Development*, http://www.uiowa.edu/ifdebook/faq/faq_docs/EMU.shtml (accessed February 27, 2010)

However, despite favorable legal structures, labor has never achieved the desirable level of mobility in the European Union. The evidence itself proves that cross-border labor mobility is devastatingly low. For example, European Central Bank (ECB) research indicated that in 2000, only .1% of the population of the EU-15 changed their official residence to another member state. By contrast, 5.9% of the US Population changed their county of residence in 1999.[3] This imbalance has continued to exist up to the present day despite legal provisions for the free movement of labor. Without the fluid movement of this fundamental factor of production, the Eurozone is deficient in an important qualification of optimal currency area. The challenge of improving labor mobility is largely cultural. Severe cultural differences rooted in the imbued nationalistic ideologies of different member states discourage workers from allocating themselves to meet market demands. Additionally, language barriers between the different member states deter cross-border collaboration and exacerbate the problems of frictional unemployment. In the United States, a common

---

[3] Heinz, F.F (2006), "Cross Border Labour Mobility Within an Enlarged EU" http://www.ecb.int/pub/pdf/scpops/ecbocp52.pdf (accessed February 27, 2010)

language and value system encourages labor movements that react to exogenous dislocations, be they in a particular geographic region or industry. In contrast, European economic shocks in a given state can often be exacerbated through long-lasting structural imbalances.

We critically delve into this divergent cultural state of the European Monetary Union, because it helps to expose another impediment that is faced in meeting the optimal currency criteria first articulated by Mundell. A hallmark of an effective union is the ability to distribute fiscal support to regions that have been adversely affected. In the United States, the federal government may pursue countercyclical policies by providing stimulus via spending in impacted states. Simultaneously, the Federal Reserve acts on a broader national level by providing liquidity and managing interest rates so as to encourage economic growth. The later case is not a viable option for the Eurozone because the stated goal of the ECB is solely to target inflation rather than growth. Yet, member states are also crippled by an inability to transfer risk through policies of fiscal redistribution. In fact, the provisions of the Stability and Growth Pact have a no-bail out clause that explicitly prohibits fiscal transfers.[4] Divergent cultural and nationalistic ideologies make assistance of other members politically untenable and disadvantageous from a self-maximization perspective. Without unity, the system is destined to collapse under the classical dichotomy of individual and collective utility in the presence of positive externalities.

On the one hand, the interconnected nature of the European countries under a currency union yields positive capabilities for combating economic shocks. The members of the Eurozone undoubtedly experience gains from increased trade. Harvard Professor Jeffrey Frankel has done extensive research indicating that countries with close links in trade tend to have business cycles that are highly correlated.[5] In theory, a common currency can allow for broader transfer of a shock, reducing the individual risk to certain nations because of collectivization. Thus, the unity of the currency region can actually help dampen shocks by transferring risk to the broader population of member states. Such interconnectedness necessarily encourages the

---

[4] Breuss, Fritz, *The stability and growth pact: experience and future aspects* (Springer 2007)

[5] Frankel, Jeffrey (1997), "The Endogeneity of the Optimum Currency Area Criteria", *The University of California, Berkeley*, http://faculty.haas.berkeley.edu/arose/ocaej.pdf (accessed February 27, 2010)

alignment of the business cycle, noted by Frankel, across member states and enables an optimal environment for coordinated countercyclical fiscal and monetary policy by the central bank. Tragically, the stringent and sole policy of inflation targeting employed by the European Central Bank fails to capitalize on the opportunities engendered by a shared economic cycle. Indeed, the promise of a stable inflationary environment was one of the primary catalysts for the formation of the Euro Area, making a policy reversal unlikely and, as we shall explore, potentially explosive for the commitment of member states to continued participation in the currency union.

In the absence of coordinated response to mitigate the effect of adverse economic conditions (as currently seen in Greek debt crisis), the collective nature of the currency union actually has an adverse effect by transforming the troubles of an individual state into a broader systemic risk. What mechanisms are in place to contain that risk from infecting the Eurozone economy? The short answer is few. As Fritz Breuss notes in his book, The Stability and Growth Pact, "Barring both default and bail-out, fiscal adjustment requires an appropriate plan of austerity."[6]

---

[6] Breuss 130

Naturally, rectifying the fiscal affairs of any nation is easier said than done. This is where the story we have traced thus far intensifies and becomes broadly relevant to the currently developing crisis.

# Foundations of Crisis

At the creation of the Euro Area, the Maastricht Treaty established several important criteria to qualify nations for admittance. Significantly, it was decided that a member state must keep its budget deficits at 3% of GDP and interest rates within 2% of the rates of the three participating countries with lowest rates.[7] Although such criteria were useful for screening potential participants, Frankel further notes a severe limitation in that "the suitability of European countries for inclusion in the EMU cannot be judged on the basis of historical data since the structure of these economies is likely to change dramatically as a result."[8] Due to shifting incentives, impositions, and constraints, it became almost impossible, ex ante, to understand the effects of admitting a nation to the currency union. Indeed, the long-term sustainability of the Euro has

---

[7] Stauffer, Amity, "What is the European Monetary Union", *The University of Iowa Center for International Finance and Development*, http://www.uiowa.edu/ifdebook/faq/faq_docs/EMU.shtml (accessed February 27, 2010)

[8] Frankel 4

been impaired by the diminished ability to predict the economic fortunes of member states far into the future.

Perhaps nowhere are the incentives for failure of the currency union more apparent than in Greece. Transitioning to the Euro was largely a coup for Greece. Beginning in 1995, and culminating with its admittance to the Economic and Monetary Union (EMU) in 2001, Greece made a concerted effort to tame inflation and meet the convergence criteria for adoption of the currency.[9] In gaining membership, Greece improved its credibility by severely decreasing its inflation and devaluation risk, leading to increases in trade and foreign direct investment. Simultaneously, decreased interest rates that accompanied the newfound economic stability enabled widespread borrowing from domestic and international sources.[10] The government was able to refinance debt on more favorable terms and the underpricing of default risk, because of the broader expansion in the credit environment, enabled low interest rates and gluttonous consumption. The economic benefits to Greece were undeniable. From 2000 to 2008, Greek GDP surged

---

[9] Burak Gundagdu and Orkun Girban (2006), "Greece's Integration to the EMU and Lessons for Turkey", *Turkish Central Bank*, http://www.tcmb.gov.tr/yeni/iletisimgm/B_Gundogdu-O_Girban.pdf (accessed March 1, 2010)

[10] Gundagdu 7

from $125 billion to $357 billion.[11] The accelerated growth in prosperity is almost identically correlated with their acceptance into the EMU in 2000 and participation starting on January 1, 2001.[12]

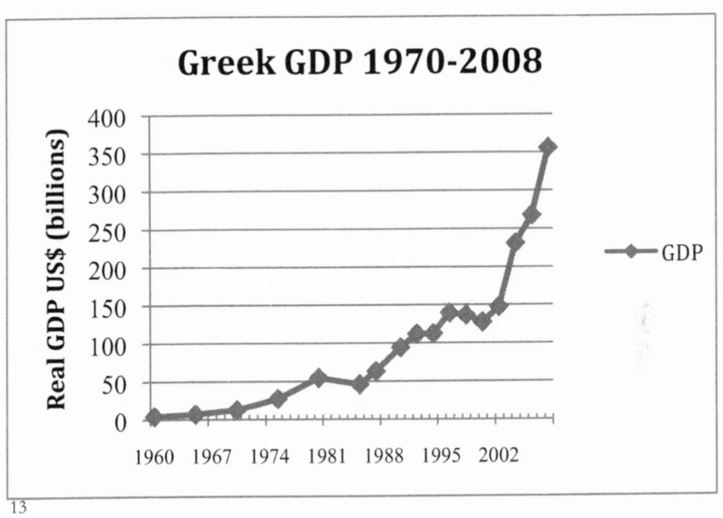


13

Between 1990 and 1999, the Greek economy grew at 2.1%, while between 2000 and 2008, with the

---

[11] Worldbank, "Key Development and Data Statistics" http://web.worldbank.org/WBSITE/EXTERNAL/DATASTATISTICS/0,,contentMDK:20535285~menuPK:1192694~pagePK:64133150~piPK:64133175~theSitePK:239419,00.html (accessed March 1, 2010)

[12] Gundagu 7

[13] World Bank, World Development Indicators, http://www.google.com/publicdata (accessed March 1, 2010)

integration of the Euro, it grew at over 4%[14]. Interestingly, the Eurozone as a whole lagged far behind in growth over the same time frame at only 1.9%. The large difference in growth rates is summarized in the following table.[15]

| Real GDP Growth Rate | 2000 | 2001 | 2002 | 2003 | 2004 | 2005 | 2006 | 2007 | 2008 | 2009 | 2010 | 2011 |
|---|---|---|---|---|---|---|---|---|---|---|---|---|
| Euro Area* | 3.9 | 1.9 | 0.9 | 0.8 | 2.1 | 1.7 | 2.9 | 2.7 | 0.6 | -4.1 | 0.7f | 1.5f |
| Greece | 4.5 | 4.2 | 3.4 | 5.9 | 4.6 | 2.2 | 4.5 | 4.5 | 2.0 | -1.1f | -0.3f | 0.7f |

*(EA11-2000, EA12-2006, EA13-2007, EA15-2008, EA16-2009)

Although this was a period of tremendous relative prosperity, the Greek government made little attempt to close its deficit or pay down its national debt. It was a classic example of failed enforcement mechanisms and confirmed the challenge of

---

14 World Bank, World Development Indicators

15 European Commission Eurostat, http://epp.eurostat.ec.europa.eu/portal/page/portal/eurostat/home/ (accessed March 2, 2010)

coordination amongst member states, effectively enabling Greek growth at the expense of the Eurozone. To be sure, the rest of the Euro Area was simultaneously engaged in an expansion of debt, but nowhere was the violation more flagrant than in prosperous Greece. Following inclusion in the EMU, the Maastricht Treaty established the Excessive Debt Procedure that "obliges Member States to comply with budgetary discipline by respecting two criteria: a deficit to GDP ratio and a debt to GDP ratio not exceeding reference values of 3% and 60% respectively,"[16] or face penalties imposed by a Council of member states. In reality, since the creation of the currency union the terms of this mandate have not been stringently enforced and countries have repeatedly violated the limits. Once Greece became a member of the EMU, its incentive to abide by the Excessive Debt Procedure was virtually eliminated.

The Greek government ceased all attempts at fiscal restraint following its inclusion in the Euro and began running ever-expanding deficits to fund its ambitious social agenda. Membership in the Euro insulated Greece from the global credit bust that began

---

16 European Commission Eurostat, "Excesive Debt Procedures" http://epp.eurostat.ec.europa.eu/portal/page/portal/government_finance_statistics/excessive_deficit (accessed March 1, 2010)

in the summer of 2007, and allowed it continued access to cheap debt markets despite a continually deteriorating fiscal outlook. By 2008 the current account deficit stood at 14.6% of GDP.[17] It is with this historical background and understanding of the failure of the Eurozone to meet the conditions of an optimal currency area that we finally engage in an analysis of the current situation. As we shall see, the realities of the present environment strongly suggest an inevitable collapse of the Euro.

---

[17] European Commission (2010), "Report on Greek Government Deficit and Debt Statistics" http://epp.eurostat.ec.europa.eu/cache/ITY_PUBLIC/COM_2010_REPORT_GREEK/EN/COM_2010_REPORT_GREEK-EN.PDF (accessed March 3, 2010)

"The goal of all of us is to leave this supervision, to leave this custody, and we won't do that with rocks or violence...it will happen when we have put our house in order."

-Greek Prime Minister George Papandreou[18]

---

[18] Wall Street Journal (April 2010), "Greek Central Banker Urges More Cuts" http://online.wsj.com/article/SB1000142405274870447120457520965168306675 6.html (accessed April 27, 2010)

# The End of the Euro

The world is currently emerging from the worst economic crisis in over half a century. Suffice to say, the system as it stands is incredibly fragile and continues to be hypersensitive, in both absolute and psychological terms, to any sort of turbulence. Confidence in the free-market system was challenged to the brink of extinction, and despite signs of resiliency and the incredibly short memories of our market participants, it is fair to assume an air of skepticism will prevail in asset prices over the medium term. It is amid this reality that we assess the unsustainable credit environment of Greece. The budget deficit stands at 12.7% of GDP, more than four times the limit established by the Maastricht Treaty.[19] Debt currently stands as 112.6% of GDP,[20] and is

---

19 Moneyweek.com (Feb 2010), "Greece: Credit Rating Slash Spooks Stocks" http://www.moneyweek.com/investments/stock-markets/greece-credit-rating-cut-46503.aspx (accessed March 3, 2010)

20 European Commission (2010), "Report on Greek Government Deficit and Debt Statistics"

projected to swell to over 125% by next year, or more than double the proposed limit from the Stability and Growth Pact.[21] There is little argument that Greece will face tremendous difficulty servicing this debt, especially since its economy is expected to contract an additional .3% this year.[22]

Add to this the absolute lack of credibility in the Greek government given the crisis of confidence over the transparency of their system. Following the elections in October, the new government revised its projection of its 2009 budget deficit from 5% to 12.7%.[23] This is hardly the first time the government has attempted to obfuscate real economic data. In 2001, the same year it gained entry to the Eurozone, Greece enlisted the help of investment banks and used currency swaps to disguise the true value of its debt with complex derivatives.[24] The measure, which amounted to a version of national accounting fraud,

---

[21] Moneyweek.com

[22] European Commission Eurostat

[23] The Economist (Feb 2010), "Greece's Soverign Debt Crunch: A very European Crisis" http://www.economist.com/world/europe/displaystory.cfm?story_id=15452594 (accessed March 3, 2010)

[24] Dalton, Mathew (Feb 2010), "EU Statistics Agency: Greek Debt Will Rise Due to 2001 Swap", *The Wall Street Journal*, http://online.wsj.com/article/BT-CO-20100224-712984.html (accessed March 3, 2010)

was not disclosed until this year. The same lack of transparency works against any Greek promises of fiscal restraint through policies of austerity. The foundations of credit are already shaky and the issues of credibility will serve only to encourage a further appreciation of financing costs for the struggling nation.

The interest rates here speak for themselves. On Thursday, February 25, Moody's issued a warning of an additional downgrade that would bring its rating in line with Fitch and Standard and Poor's who have already downgraded long-term Greek Sovereign debt to B ratings.[25] Inevitably, Moody's will, despite its present stance, drop its rating to Baa1 and Greece will no longer be able to exchange its loans as collateral with the European Central Bank, a mechanism which has long served as an important source of financing. This will place additional constraints on Greek access to credit markets and raise the cost of servicing debt. The rate on two-year bonds has already soared to near 7% and the spread over the benchmark German Bund has

---

25 Oakley, David (Feb 2010), "Moody's joins S&P in warning on Greece" http://www.ft.com/cms/s/0/a88ef798-21f9-11df-98dd-00144feab49a.html (accessed March 3, 2010)

continued to widen to around 4%.[26]

The overwhelming Greek deficit and debt makes it the lynchpin among members of the Eurozone, but it is only the tip of the iceberg in terms of escalating debt crises. Portugal is close behind in the erosion of confidence and has seen its spread over the Bund widen almost a full percentage point over the past month. Spain and Ireland both boast budget deficits in excess of 10% of GDP. Even more troublesome is Italy's debt to GDP ratio of 114.6%. Italy's economy alone is more than three times the size of Greece, Portugal, and Ireland combined. Yet, the current focus and the bulk of our analysis rests sharply on Greece, and rightly so. The situation in Greece is holding the floodgates of the debt crisis and will undoubtedly set the precedent for European affairs going forward. The first test will come with come in April when the Greeks will need to refinance around €22 billion of debt that comes due([27]).

Furthermore, interest rates are already artificially low thanks to drastic rate cutting undertaken by the ECB in the wake of the global economic devastation of

---

[26] Oakley, David (Feb 2010), "Moody's joins S&P in warning on Greece"

[27] The Economist (Feb 2010), "Greece's Soverign Debt Crunch: A very European Crisis" (all approximations in this paragraph)

the last two years. Signs of inflation have already begun creeping back into the Eurozone and the ECB will inevitably have to take further measures to withdraw the unprecedented liquidity from the system at some point in the future. This will raise rates from the 1% where they have remained for the past 10 months, driving up the cost of financing, and significantly constraining the ability of fragile economies such as Greece to raise debt.[28]

The prospects for recovery through growth and cost cutting are also bleak. The primary defense currently being considered by many nations involves a reduction of deficits to sustainable levels. Greece has proposed a series of austerity measures to close the budget gap, but the bond markets have continued to price these measures with increasing skepticism. Our own experience with slashing the size of government here in the United States hardly begins to match the challenges the Eurozone faces in rolling back excessive spending. The culture of "socialism," is much more pervasive and spending cuts will result in widespread political backlash that further upsets the stability of

---

28 The Associated Press (Mar 2010), "ECB Holds Rates, Withdrawing Some Crisis Measures" http://www.nytimes.com/aponline/2010/03/04/business/AP-EU-Europe-Interest-Rates.html (accessed March 4, 2010)

countries. Greeks for example have in the past enjoyed a pension that is 96% of pre-retirement earnings.[29] Simultaneously, the looming threats of an aging population and escalating health care costs remain ever present. This devastating long-term fiscal outlook stands in conjunction with a potentially contracting supply of loanable funds from savers. Europe cannot continue to rely on foreign savers such as the Chinese to fund their markets for debt, especially if depreciating currency reverses the flow of Eurozone demand for imports, reduces the attractiveness of its bonds, and places further pressure on interest rates.

By definition, the ECB must confront one of two options. For one, it can eventually raise rates via its current mandate as we have already suggested. This not only increases the costs of raising and refinancing debt in struggling nations but also places continual strain on the growth of their output. One way the higher rates accomplish this is by making investment more difficult. They also serve as an indirect support for currency and make export driven growth more challenging. This case surely has an adverse effect on Greece and makes default all the more likely. The

---

[29] The Economist (Feb 2010), "Greece's Soverign Debt Crunch: A very European Crisis"

Greek perspective favors low interest rates to maintain cheap credit and a weaker Euro that will drive its export sector and boost savings by closing its current account deficit. Indeed exports account for 22% of Greek GDP.[30] All else equal, Greece would prefer to instate its own weaker currency and make this option viable. But we hardly need to concern ourselves over whether the defection of Greece, or any weak country for that matter, will pose a threat to the continued use of the Euro. They can never dump the Euro in favor of reinstating their own depreciated currency because their existing debt obligations are still denominated in Euros and doing so would only make the situation more miserable by increasing the real size of the debt burden.

In the United States we can inflate or "print" our way out of any deficit because our debt is denominated in dollars, but this is not true for participants in the European Currency Union. Moreover, the mere appearance of abandoning the Euro in favor of a restored depreciated national currency would cause widespread panic in a debt-burdened nation such as

---

30 Worldbank, "Key Development and Data Statistics" http://web.worldbank.org/WBSITE/EXTERNAL/DATASTATISTICS/0,,contentMDK:20535285~menuPK:1192694~pagePK:64133150~piPK:64133175~theSitePK:239419,00.html (accessed March 3, 2010)

Greece, leading to bank runs, capital flight, as well as a devastatingly severe drop in asset prices. In nations that have floating exchange rates, the increase in country risk reduces the value of their domestic currency. This risk premium may impose a higher nominal interest rate, but real interest rate fluctuations are often dampened by a parallel increase in inflationary expectations. All else equal, a country with a higher nominal interest rate can be expected to undergo an exchange rate depreciation and a country with a lower nominal interest rate can be expected to undergo an exchange rate appreciation. In the floating exchange rate regime, a shock in country risk is partially, if not totally, mitigated by the stimulation of the export sector at a lower real exchange rate.

Greece and the Eurozone do not have the luxury of this option. The exchange rate of the Euro is largely fixed by factors such as ECB policy and the economic environment of the largest Eurozone states. Without the benefit of a depreciating national currency, Greece's economy is placed in a disequilibrium that will take many years to correct. A decrease in price levels is necessary to circumvent the problem of a "fixed" exchange rate by similarly lowering the price of Greek output. Since the nation can't rely on expansionary ECB monetary policy to stimulate the economy and lower the price of its goods, the price of those goods will have to fall in absolute terms for any given money supply. This deflationary process will prove to be extremely painful, slowing already anemic growth and substantially increasing the size of Greece's real debt burden. Any subsequent contractions in Eurozone money supply will serve only to bolster the trade-weighted value of the Euro, reducing Greek competitiveness, and exacerbating the size of their deflationary pressures.

On the one hand the ECB can raise rates, raise the likelihood of a default by Greece and others, and maintain its inflation-targeting mandate, or the ECB can break from that precedent and maintain depressed interest rates in an attempt to stimulate the economies of struggling member states. Such a strategy would reduce the burden of debt and drive revival through economic vitality as mentioned, but it would come at the cost of debasing the very foundations of the European Central Bank and Economic and Monetary Union. The Maastricht Treaty was predicated, at the insistence of Germany, on a commitment to a stable currency and price level. Germany also insisted upon the no-bailout provision in order to make the adoption of the Euro tenable for its skeptical population.[31] Fast-forward to 2010 and those very promises are being compromised as a German-led bailout of Greece sits high on the list of probabilities.

There is no reason to assume that Germany must shrink into the corner and renege on its promise to not bail out the weaker states. The German economy is far and away the largest in the Eurozone, accounting for over a quarter of its output. Although a beacon of strength, Germany also has its own sizeable domestic debt commitments that would impair its ability to bailout other countries. For 2009, Germany's debt to GDP ratio spiked to 77.2%, well in excess of the Eurozone limit, and its deficit is projected to rise to 5% of GDP.[32] Suppose it wasn't Greece that departed from the currency union, but rather Germany. The reinvented Deutschemark would rise not fall, reducing the burden of debt denominated in Euros and make all Euro-priced assets, from equities to real estate, even cheaper for the Germans to buy than they already are.[33]

---

[31] Breuss, Fritz, *The stability and growth pact: experience and future aspects* (Springer 2007)

[32] CIA World Factbook, "Germany" https://www.cia.gov/library/publications/the-world-factbook/geos/gm.html (accessed March 4, 2010)

[33] Webb, Merryn (Feb 2010), "Why Germany should dump the Euro", *Moneyweek.com*, http://www.moneyweek.com/blog/why-

Simultaneously, they gain the advantage of price stability and release themselves from the grips of a wayward ECB. Additionally, the move would certainly be more appealing to many German taxpayers than bailing out their irresponsible Eurozone neighbors. So the incentives for a German departure are clearly in place should the ECB decide to break its mandate as a means to combat the debt crisis. If Germany were to depart the currency union the credibility of the Euro would be irreparably destroyed, along with any commitment by the central banks to tame inflation or of member states to exercise fiscal restraint. To be sure, the probability of this scenario, in my view, remains highly unlikely since it would virtually ensure the destruction of the Euro.

Thus, it is fair to assume that in all likelihood the ECB will stick to its mandate, increasing pressure on debt-ridden nations such as Greece via the mechanisms we have already discussed and further weakening the prospects of recovery through growth, exports, and fiscal restraint. This course of action can lead the Eurozone in only two directions, both nearly equally dismal. The first, and currently consensus option, is

---

germany-should-dump-the-euro-00122.aspx (accessed March 4, 2010)

that states of relative strength, namely Germany and France, show solidarity and make sacrifices through bailout to eliminate a potential systemic risk. As in past fiscal crises, a loan program would be established in conjunction with the International Monetary Fund. Although the action might temporarily mitigate the negative externalities of a Greek default, it would spell political disaster for the already narrow margins of Nicolas Sarkozy and Angela Merkel who are up for reelection in 2012 and 2013 respectively.[34]

But more significantly, it is my view that any type of bailout would establish an overwhelming moral hazard that would doom the future of the currency union. Throughout history, for example, the option of IMF loans and bailouts has consistently had an adverse effect on the capacity of central governments to reign in deficits. The immense public opposition to spending cuts has incited riots against Greek austerity plans at precisely the time when such reductions in spending are required to lower the nation's risk premium.

The bailout of Greece would come at the expense of further instability by encouraging reckless fiscal behavior. In absolute terms, the size of the

---

[34] CIA Worldfactbook, "Germany and France" https://www.cia.gov/library/publications/the-world-factbook/geos.html (accessed March 4, 2010)

Greek debt burden is small and could be absorbed by the solidarity of the Eurozone powerhouses, but on the peripheral are the insurmountable collective debts of Portugal, Ireland, Italy, and Spain. Italy's debt burden for example is more than five times as large as Greece's.[35] By bailing out Greece, Germany and France would establish a precedent that would open the floodgates for a much larger future crisis. In the long term, violating the provisions of the no-bailout clause and upsetting the accords of the Maastricht Treaty would almost certainly result in the break up of the currency union. It is already evident that enforcement mechanisms on debt levels are all too easily ignored and that faith in a member state's promise is useless, especially when there is no viable option for the departure or eviction of weak states from the currency union. The path of bailout leads only to further reckless fiscal spending, an exacerbated debt crisis, long-term instability, and political upheaval in the stronger Eurozone member states.

35 Worldbank, "Key Development and Data Statistics"

# The Greek Default

This leaves us with the final alternative: default. The devastation of a default by Greece and others would have almost unimaginable consequences for the vitality of the EMU. It is this threat of default that makes a bailout led by power states and the IMF tenable. A Greek default would raise the cost of borrowing for other troubled Eurozone members to unsustainable levels. The skyrocketing costs of capital would be coupled with an erosion of confidence and plummet in the Euro far beyond the 10% drop it has experienced over the past three months.[36] Strong countries such as Germany would see increased incentives for departure and ultimately threaten the stability of the currency union. Existing debt burdens would be severely exacerbated by the lethal combination of rising rates and a falling currency.

---

36 XRates.com, "Euro to 1 USD" http://www.xrates.com/d/EUR/USD/graph120.html (accessed March 4, 2010)

A Greek default is also a viable option in the event that the size of the loan package mustered by the IMF and European leader states fails to prevent contagion. Portugal would likely be the next country to go under. The holders of deteriorating bonds, the majority of whom are within the Eurozone, would similarly suffer from the appreciation of rates. The spike in spreads over the German Bund for the troubled nations has reached an alarming scale over the past month, with 10 year Irish and Portuguese debt both trading at over 100 basis points over the Bund, and Greek debt reaching a spread of nearly 400 basis points seen in the following figure.[37] If self-fulfilling prophecies set in, the jump in credit spreads may prove overwhelming to any sort of coordinated response by the Eurozone. Even if an initial bailout package were large enough to stave off the Greek default, it would come nowhere near the size requisite to contain the subsequent sovereign debt crises in other member states.

---

[37] Thomson Reuters, *The Economist (Feb 2010),* "Greece's Soverign Debt Crunch: A very European Crisis"

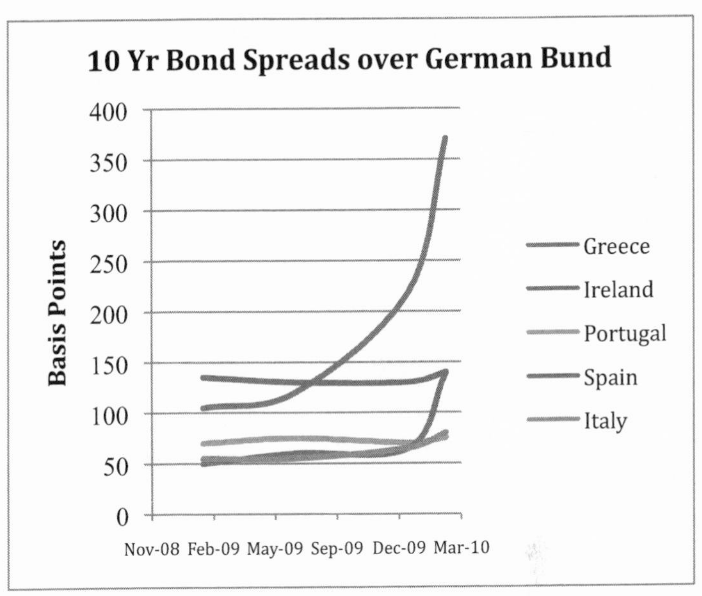


The realities of the market outlook on the increasing probabilities of default speak for themselves. Credit default swap (CDS) prices on the sovereign debts of struggling nations are exploding to troubling levels. The annual cost protecting against default of Greece has risen four-fold over the past six months to around 4%.[38] On February 24th, the cost of insuring a €10,000,000 obligation of 5-year Greek debt stood at €382,000 a year, compared with less than €100,000 as

[38] Thomson Reuters, "Global Soverign Credit Default Swaps" http://blogs.reuters.com/rolfe-winkler/files/2010/02/kyd77h.jpg (accessed March 4, 2010)

late as August of 2009.[39] Portuguese and Spanish sovereign debt has experienced an erosion of confidence of a similar magnitude over this time period.

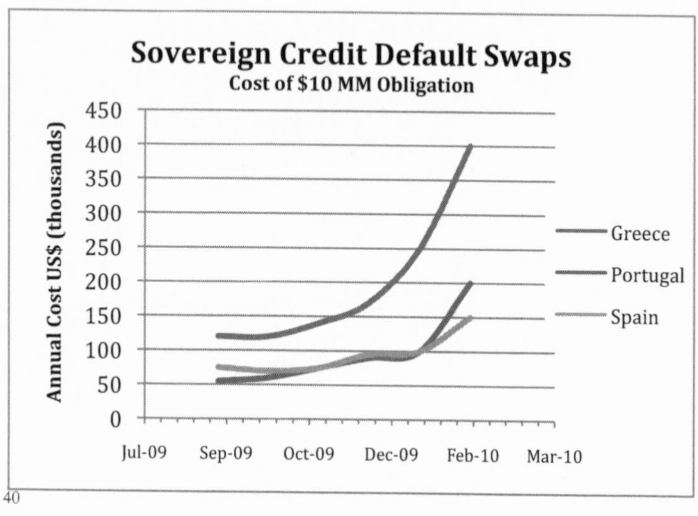

[40]

The time frame and levels of the cost protection in the CDS market for select European sovereign debt looks eerily similar to the experience of Lehman Brothers before its default in September of 2008. Lehman's CDS prices appreciated fairly steadily before

---

[39] Bloomberg, "Greek Bonds Slide as Debt Concerns Pushes Up Premium Over Bunds" http://www.bloomberg.com/apps/news?pid=20601009&sid=avNkHG1eWlF4 (accessed March 4, 2010)

[40] Thomson Reuters, "Global Soverign Credit Default Swaps"

fully exploding in cost during the days leading up to collapse.[41]

Indeed, the comparison to the financial crisis is very fitting because the current environment in Europe is akin to the insolvency troubles investment banks faced in 2008, only played out with governments on a transnational scale in 2010. The high debt levels, as a percentage of GDP, are comparable to the leveraged balance sheets of Wall Street banks. The fiscal difficulties faced by governments and their decrease in revenues during the economic downturn mirrors the losses and writedowns taken at financial institutions. The most highly leveraged institutions were more severely impacted, just as the countries with high deficit and debt ratios are most challenged by the costs of financing and servicing debt. I draw this comparison at length because it emphasizes another major point. What matters most in any credit crisis is confidence. In his book, House of Cards, William Cohan details the tragic and theoretically unnecessary collapse of Bear Stearns. [42] The enormous capital cushion of Bear Stearns in February of 2008 was not sufficient to

---

41 Noelwatson.com, "Lehman CDS" http://www.noelwatson.com/blog/content/binary/LehmanCDS29012009.gif (accessed March 5, 2010)

42 Cohan, William, *House of Cards: A Tale of Hubris and Wretched Excess on Wall Street* (Doubleday 2009)

combat their perceived insolvency and the mismanagement of their financial condition. Despite being profitable its final quarter, and operating a functioning business model, Bear suffered from the ever-increasing collateral demands of creditors. In the world of finance, as in the global capital markets, perceptions become realities and often serve as a sort of self-fulfilling prophecy. The demands of Greece's creditors are no different in that they can drive up the cost of borrowing irrespective of the fundamental realities of their future fiscal condition and commitments. It is for this reason that we cannot rely solely on projections and theory in determining the sustainability of Greek debt and indeed the broader European currency area.

Greece is every bit as susceptible to an attack by financial speculation as was Bear Stearns. Hedge funds have already begun a wave of short positions on the Euro and European debt.[43] Yet, unlike the isolated threat of a single investment bank, the systemic risk here is much broader because there does not exist a central authority to coordinate containment and relief as the United States government did in response to the

---

[43] Jones, Sam (Feb 2010), "Hedge fund prosper from Greek debt", *Financial Times*, http://www.ft.com/cms/s/0/a6b71b50-249f-11df-8be0-00144feab49a.html (accessed March 5 2010)

financial crisis. Because the Eurozone is an amalgamation of divergent political states, the bailout of Greece promises to be much more challenging.

Furthermore, the precedent set by the U.S. government in February 2008 when it chose to bailout Bear Stearns is largely attributed as a significant influence in the September collapse of Lehman Brothers. Just as a Greek bailout would encourage other countries such as Portugal to believe they had a similar safety net, so too was Lehman Brothers convinced that the Federal Government would step in to save it. Dick Fuld, the CEO of Lehman was stunned when Treasury Secretary Hank Paulson, "Pulled the fire alarm…There will be no bailout for Lehman."[44] It was the bankruptcy of Lehman that finally set off the full-blown financial meltdown that the United States and the world experienced. Like Bear Stearns, Greece may choose to flaunt its nuclear card and force the assistance of neighboring states to mitigate a systemic risk. Through "bailout," Eurozone members would back current Greek debt in order facilitate a transition to austerity, just as the U.S. government guaranteed Bear's obligations to facilitate an acquisition by JP Morgan. Ultimately, it may not be

---

[44] Cohan 434

Greek default that tips the scale of fortune for the Eurozone. However, we can be certain that the permanent moral hazard established through a bailout will encourage continued abusive fiscal policies that will severely cripple the long-term sustainability of the Euro.

"Bond-market vigilantes already have taken aim at Greece, Spain, Portugal, the United Kingdom, Ireland, and Iceland, pushing government bond yields higher…Eventually they may take aim at other countries – even Japan and the United States -- where fiscal policy is on an unsustainable path."

-Nouriel Roubini, Professor of Economics at NYU Stern School of Business and Chairman of Roubini Global Economics[45]

[45] CNBC (April 2010), "Greece Just Tip of Debt Crisis Iceberg: Roubini" http://classic.cnbc.com/id/36795861/ (accessed April 27, 2010)

# European Monetary Union Conclusion

In conclusion, we have seen that the Eurozone fails to meet many of the criteria for an optimum currency area because of deep-rooted cultural differences and an inability to capitalize on the efficiencies of the currency union to combat shocks via a fiscal transfer mechanism. Simultaneously, the inflation-targeting mandate of the ECB has severely constricted the ability of Europe to respond to crisis. We forecasted that in all likelihood the ECB would stick to this mandate, rather than risk upsetting the foundations of the Maastricht Treaty. Pursuing a policy of inflation and currency depreciation would help debt-ridden nations such as Greece, but virtually ensure the defection of powerful member states such as Germany from the currency union. Instead, the ECB will stick by its stated mandate and will eventually be forced to drain liquidity and raise rates, adversely impacting the ability of Greece to pay down debt. This environment comes about as a direct result of the failure of the Eurozone to meet the requirements of an optimal currency area because of a divergent political unity. We established that under this scenario prospects for Greek growth and exports would be further constrained by higher costs of capital, low inflation, and a stronger currency. Thus, we are left with only two options for Greece, a bailout or default.

The bailout introduces incentives for continued fiscal mismanagement in other struggling member states and will prompt a domino effect that will eventually drag the debt burdens of larger nations into crises beyond the scope that is rectifiable by coordinated reaction to systemic risk. This is the more likely option and in the long run will result in the inevitable collapse of the Euro. Conversely, the alternative is to permit Greece to default. This would thrash the Euro and drive up the costs of financing, further eroding the credit ratings of other nations struggling to reduce their debt burdens. Once initiated, the catastrophic spiral of this erosion of confidence would guide the Eurozone down the same path of collapse experienced by investment banks during the great financial crisis of 2008. Starting in Portugal, successive defaults would spread into a broader systemic failure that magnifies the incentives of powerful states to defect from the union in favor of stronger and nation-specific currencies. Similarly, we were able to draw parallels between the realities inherent in the spreads of Eurozone sovereign debt over the Bund and the spike in member state CDS, with the increasing demands of collateral and erosion of confidence that was reflected in the history of Bear Stearns and Lehman Brothers. We also identified within the financial crisis, the danger of a precedent through bailout, which can now be applied to the predicament posed by Greece. Ultimately, we inevitably face Greek bailout or default and both scenarios lead to the collapse of the Euro.

# PART TWO

*Grant Wonders*
*May 2010*

---

## The Perils of Global Imbalance

---

*Grant Wonders*
*May 2010*

# Beginning of an Era

The breakdown of the Bretton Woods system of monetary management has made the U.S. dollar the world's de-facto reserve currency. In mid-August of 1971, President Nixon called his top economic advisers to his retreat at Camp David and devised the most momentous policy change in the history of international economics.[46] Over a weekend the administration moved to eliminate fixed exchange rates and broke the peg of the U.S. dollar by going off the gold standard. Eschewing the obligation of convertibility and transitioning to a fiat currency allowed the U.S. to begin assuming deficits without fear of draining its gold reserves. By stimulating the short-

[46]Daniel Yergin and Joseph Stanislaw (1997), "Commanding Heights: Nixon Tries Price Controls", *PBS*, http://www.pbs.org/wgbh/commandingheights/shared/minitextlo/ess_nixongold.html (accessed April 26, 2010)

term economy and implementing politically popular price controls, Nixon was able to win the election of 1972 by one of the largest margins in history, sweeping every single state except for Massachusetts, and gaining over 60% of the popular vote.[47] The action may have helped Nixon's short-term politics, but it also introduced a long-term mechanism for one of the most significant global economic threats in world history.

---

[47] Our Campagins, "US President National Vote Race Details – Nov 07, 1972" http://www.ourcampaigns.com/RaceDetail.html?RaceID=1939 (accessed April 26, 2010)

"Philosophically, however, I was still against wage-price controls, even though I was convinced that the objective reality of the economic situation forced me to impose them."

-President Richard Nixon[48]

[48] Daniel Yergin and Joseph Stanislaw (1997), "Commanding Heights: Nixon Tries Price Controls"

# Decline of Gold and Rise of Imbalance

The financial crisis aside, most would characterize the decades since the transition to the dollar standard as a time of relatively high American prosperity. But the period has also been marked by a tremendous accumulation of global imbalances and rampant expansion of credit. The collapse of the gold standard ushered in an era of asset bubbles and a perpetual overaccumulation of personal, corporate, and sovereign debt. The world as a whole is overleveraged in an unsustainable economic system. Signs of strain have already begun to emerge. For now, Greece has captured the spotlight as a poster child for imbalance and excessive debt, with global markets keenly interpreting Europe's reaction to the ongoing crisis. The fiscal positions of peripheral countries, including Portugal and Spain, are also looking increasingly tenuous as communicated by the surging cost of default protection. Greek sovereign debt has opened a spread of nearly 7% over the 10-year German bund, and the spread for Portuguese debt has similarly surged to around 3%.[49] However, the currently developing challenges of Greece and Europe are only the beginning of a larger threat that lurks on the horizon. The crash following the burst of the U.S. real estate bubble marks the beginning of more significant challenges for American credit. The current account deficits of the United States are increasingly unsustainable. Inevitably, the global imbalances that have emerged under the dollar standard must be restored to equilibrium. As we will develop in the in the remainder of this book, the inexorable fall of the dollar is fast becoming imminent.

Undeniably, the dollar (the Euro to a lesser extent, especially given the current environment) has been held as the reserve currency of choice since the decline of the gold standard. The implicit "stability" of the American greenback has enabled the United States to issue debt and engage in irresponsible fiscal action to a far greater extent than would have been possible did it not enjoy such a preferred status. The ability of the

---

[49] Landon Thomas and Nicholas Kulish (Apr 2010), "I.M.F. Promises More Aid for Greece as European Crisis Grows", *The New York Times*, http://www.nytimes.com/2010/04/29/business/global/29euro.html?hp (accessed April 27, 2010)

fiat dollar to maintain strength despite surging national debt and sustained current account deficits is truly remarkable. The U.S. current account is approximately equal to the balance of trade, but also includes net international factor income, such as remittances by an American working abroad, and net unilateral transfer payments, such as U.S. aid to Haiti. Since the current account was last positive in 1991, the cumulative deficit has accumulated more than $6.9 trillion.[50] It has also exceeded $300 billion every year since 1999. Over this time frame, the dollar has also preserved most of its value against a basket of major currencies. The ICE U.S. Dollar Index (USDX) fell only around 12% from 93.96 at the start of 1999 to around 83 as of April 2010.[51] Ironically, much of the relative prosperity sustained as a result of deficits has and will continue to exacerbate the scale of the inexorable collapse on the horizon.

In taking a pessimistic stance on the global economic climate under a paper dollar regime, I run the

---

50 Bureau of Economic Analysis, "U.S. International Transactions Accounts Data" http://www.bea.gov/international/bp_web/list.cfm?anon=71®istered=0 (accessed April 28, 2010)

51 IntercontinentalExchange, "ICE U.S. Dollar Index (USDX)" https://www.theice.com/productguide/ProductGroupHierarchy.shtml?groupDetail=&group.groupId=17 (accessed April 28, 2010)

risk of misleading the reader into believing that the halcyon days of the gold standard were somehow superior. To be sure, I categorically oppose a monetary system backed by gold. Under the Bretton Woods system, inherent stabilization mechanisms would have made huge budget and trade deficits impossible to sustain. For example, a negative trade balance would lead to the outflow of gold reserves and require the United States government to take action to rectify the trade balance in order to avoid recession. Since every dollar is backed by gold under the Bretton Woods system, outflow of the commodity, if left unchecked, would otherwise require the government to withdraw currency from circulation. That reduction of money supply would result in economic contraction that would similarly rectify the balance of trade. With the removal of Bretton Woods, the United States could make payments abroad without gold, or even a currency backed by gold. The automatic adjustment mechanism was gone and the United States was free to pay for its imports with pure paper dollars or their electronic equivalents. Moreover, as the privileged backer of the world's preferred reserve currency the U.S. enjoys the luxury of being able to issue debt instruments that are denominated in their currency. This gives the United States government the ability to take on unprecedented levels of debt with no concern of default and provides immense advantages in the global capital markets.

Nonetheless, currencies backed by gold, or any commodity, have their own set of deal breaking roadblocks. For one, the expansion of underlying supply can be too sporadic, leading to conflicting and entirely unpredictable inflationary or deflationary expectations. The inflexible money supply also reduces the ability of the government and central bank to combat shocks with fiscal and monetary policy. This necessarily prevents Keynesian responses from functioning, thus exacerbating fluctuations and potentially promoting instability. We observed this previously when looking at the Europe, where the ECB policy of strict inflation-targeting reduces the flexibility of the money supply. This prevents the engineering of inflation that might, for example, combat the Greek crisis by reducing their sovereign debt burden. Moreover, the ability of a Eurozone central authority to encourage transfers that combat economic shocks is largely constrained by monetary stability just as it would be for a deficit-ridden nation under the gold standard. Tragically, beyond these negative traits the Europea Currency Union shares with a commodity regir also further possesses many of the same tendencies towards leverage as the dollar. Clearly, the lack of unlimited Euro printing power has not prevented nations across the Eurozone from accumulating severe debt burdens.

With the growth of debt coming from import nations, such as the U.S. (and their resulting deficits) export nations such as China have developed counterbalancing surpluses. Foreign countries have become dependent on the U.S. as an export market for their goods. Their economies are marked by overcapacity and rely on exporting to the United States in far greater numbers than they import. Simultaneously, those foreign exporters have been accumulating reserves not in gold, but primarily in dollar-denominated debt instruments. The surplus nations have two main options for the dollars they receive from their sales abroad. They can convert them to into their domestic currency and invest within their country. Such action would contribute to an appreciation by bidding up the trade-weighted value of the domestic currency and simultaneously depreciating the value of the dollar. This harms the competitiveness of the surplus nation's industries through the lethal combination of making its goods more expensive in conjunction with a weaker American consumer base, thus adversely impacting the strategy of export-driven growth. Conversely, they can hold the reserves in dollars, or more specifically, invest them in dollar-denominated assets that will earn a positive return. For example, they might purchase United States Treasury Securities. In February 2010, China singlehandedly held $878 billion in notes, bills, and bonds, accounting for around a quarter of all outstanding treasury debt.[52] The United States is able to finance an enormous trade deficit by issuing debt, so long as counterparties in surplus nations are willing to hold U.S. debt as a reserve asset. This substitution of financial instruments to settle current account deficits has enabled a cumulative deficit of over $7.84 trillion since Bretton Woods collapsed in 1973.[53]

As Brandon Adams notes in *The Setting Sun: The End of U.S. Economic Dominance*, the expansion in trade that has been sustained by continual deficits has been "mutually beneficial."[54] The U.S. has been able to fund its consumption at negative real rates (given our inflationary future), while developing surplus nations

---

[52] United States Treasury Department, "Major Holders of Treasury Securities" http://www.treas.gov/tic/mfh.txt (accessed April 28, 2010)

[53] Bureau of Economic Analysis, "U.S. International Transactions Accounts Data"

[54] Adams, Brandon, *The Setting Sun: The End of US Economic Dominance* (Publishing Pending 2010)

have attained prosperity through export-driven growth. United States imports have steadily risen since 1973, while exports have struggled to fill in the gap.

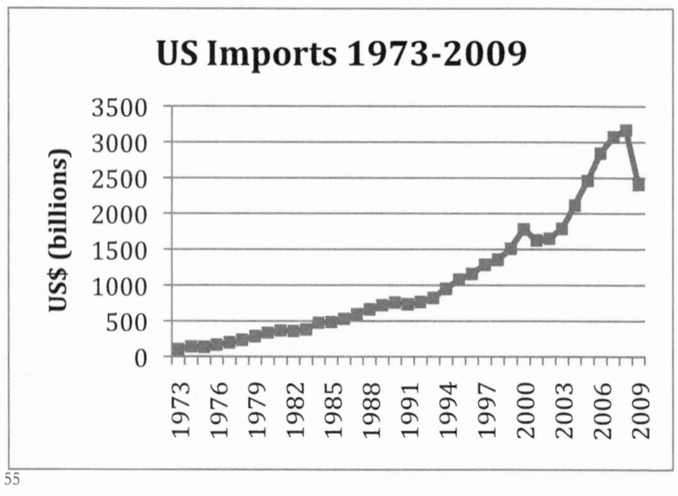


55

The imports of goods and services as well as foreign income payments have far outstripped the increase in the exports of goods and services combined with foreign income receipts. The imbalance is reflected in the diversion of the import line above the export line as seen in the following chart. During this time period, America was consuming beyond its production and borrowed to finance the difference.

[55] Bureau of Economic Analysis, "U.S. International Transactions Accounts Data"

This has resulted in the accumulation of a massive trade deficit in parallel that is largely responsible for the string of current account deficits.

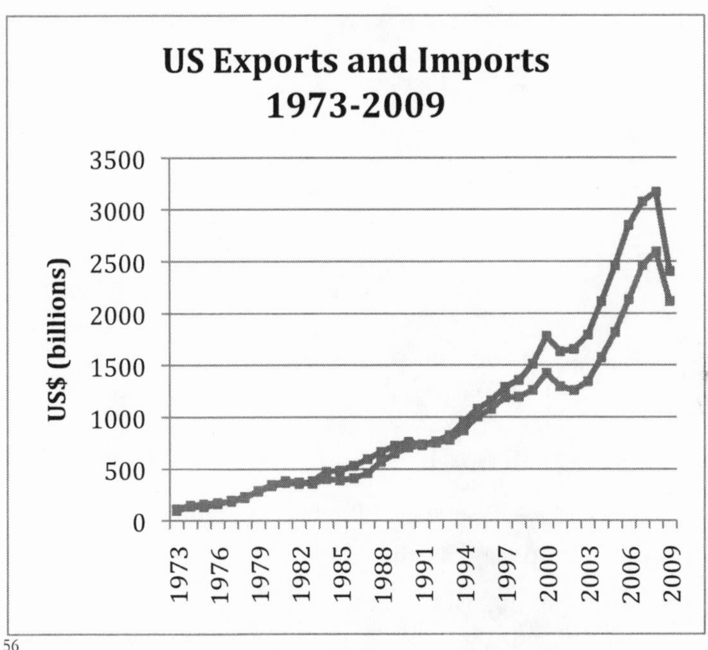

[56]

[56] Bureau of Economic Analysis, "U.S. International Transactions Accounts Data"

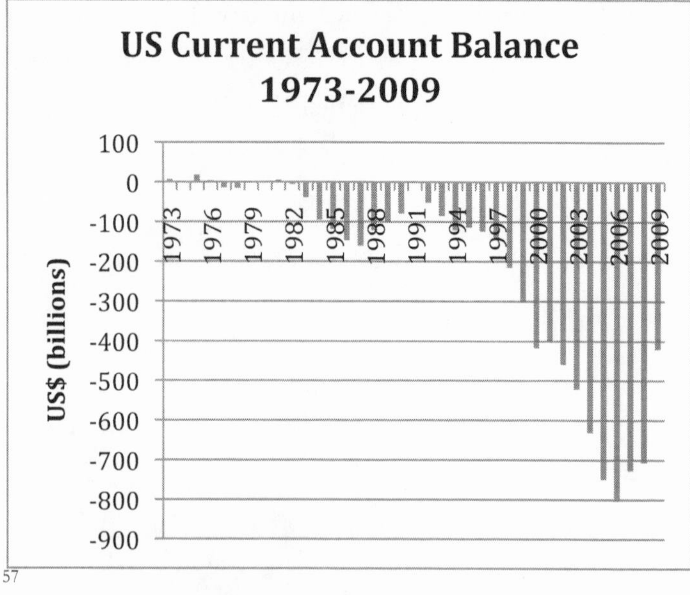


[57]

The deficit in the current account is offset by a surplus in the capital or financial account. The irony of the situation is that the United States is able to buy more from the world than it sells, and finances this with dollars backed by pure paper. Inevitably, these dollars return to the United States to earn interest by purchasing assets that are dollar-denominated. The overwhelming majority of the foreign inflow shows up as a surplus in the financial account that almost exactly counterbalances the current account deficit. The return

---

[57] Bureau of Economic Analysis, "U.S. International Transactions Accounts Data"

of these dollars by preference and necessity has helped to propel the widespread appreciation of stock and real estate markets, especially since the early 1990s. It has also managed to fund the expansion of United States public, private, and corporate debt at favorable rates of interest. Superficially, the imbalance has been positive: export-driven growth continues primarily in the developing world, global asset prices rise, rates on debt remain low, and the United States (which is responsible for more than 57% of global cumulative current account deficits)[58] is able to enjoy prolonged consumption beyond its means.

58 International Monetary Fund, "IMF World Economic Outlook Database" http://www.imf.org/external/pubs/ft/weo/2009/01/weodata/index.aspx (accessed April 29, 2010)

# The Perils of Asset Bubbles

However, as with all inefficient economic outcomes, the imbalance is also accompanied by a tradeoff. Countries with significant surpluses generate a bubble economy with tremendous overcapacity and production ability outstrips domestic consumers. Outsized demand for both their assets and products perpetuates a surplus that eventually pops and leaves the once high-growth economy in shambles. This was exactly the path followed by Japan starting in the early 1980s. Beginning in 1981, they began running successive trade surpluses.[59] At first Japan was able to export capital by buying foreign financial assets at a pace roughly equally to the accumulation of its current account surplus, thus resulting in an approximate balance of flows. By 1985, the financial account deficit was no longer growing at a pace significant enough to counterbalance the current account surplus and their

[59] Duncan, Richard, *The Dollar Crisis: Causes, Consequences, Cures* (Wiley 2003)

overall balance of payments reached nearly $50 billion by 1987.[60] As a result, the surpluses entered the banking system, much like high-powered money, and Japan's mounting international reserves enabled an increase in money supply and an expanding credit environment. Via the multiplier effect, the expansion would encourage severe appreciation in asset prices and an overheated economy. As the decade closed, the Imperial Gardens of Tokyo were valued at more than all the property in California.[61] The asset bubble also encouraged a misallocation of resources and set the stage for the structural issues that would plague the Japanese economy in the following decade. Once the bubble finally pops, the export-driven and surplus nation falls victim to severe credit contraction that disrupts the banking system, throws it into recession, and leaves it immensely oversupplied in a prolonged stagnant economic condition.

Interestingly, foreign capital inflow can impose these detrimental asset bubbles on an economy regardless of whether it enters through a trade surplus (as was the case in Japan) or a financial account surplus

---

[60] International Monetary Fund, "International Monetary Statistics Trial" http://www.imfstatistics.org/imf/ (accessed April 29, 2010)
[61] Duncan, Richard, *The Dollar Crisis: Causes, Consequences, Cures, P. 25* (Wiley 2003)

(as the United States is currently experiencing). The asset bubble in the United States arose not because of a current account surplus, but rather, a deficit. Foreign surplus nations have used their positive current accounts to buy U.S. government bonds, agency debt, corporate debt, and stocks, as evidenced by the surge in the balance of the financial account. Inevitably, this inflow of capital entered the banking system and ignited an expansion of credit that was exacerbated by the multiplier effect. By investment in corporate bonds and equity issues, foreign inflow helped to facilitate a misallocation of capital. A classic example of this structural imbalance was the technology bubble of the late 1990s in which now defunct dot.coms dominated markets for capital. When that bubble burst, equity markets swooned and the U.S. economy moved towards recession. The NASDAQ lost more than 74% of its value falling from an all time high of 5132.52 during trading on March 10, 2000 to only 1335.51 by the close of 2002.[62]

This shock, followed by further destabilization on September 11, 2001, threatened to contract credit in the United States and precipitate a correction in global

62 Yahoo! Finance, "NASDAQ Composite (^IXIC) Historical Prices" http://finance.yahoo.com/q/hp?s=%5EIXIC (accessed April 28, 2010)

imbalances. It is quite possible that an acute recession in 2001 would have dampened demand for foreign imports. If the engine for world growth had seized up and halted its expansion of debt back in 2001, the dollar would have collapsed, world export-driven growth would have plummeted, and declines in foreign inflows would have accompanied a reversal of the current account deficit that stood around $400 billion.[63] To be sure, pain would have been severe from a global correction of imbalances.

Like Greece today, the United States in 2001 was highly leveraged. Total credit market debt, both public and private, in the U.S. of around $27 trillion was nearly three times the size of its GDP.[64] A declining economy would have reduced personal income, corporate profits, and government inflows, exacerbating the size of the existing debt burden. Simultaneously, deflationary pressures exerted by structural imbalances and oversupply, once coupled with waning demand, would have encouraged even more aggressive fiscal and monetary policy once the

---

63 Bureau of Economic Analysis, "U.S. International Transactions Accounts Data"

64 Federal Reserve, "Flow of Funds: Credit Market Debt Outstanding" http://www.federalreserve.gov/releases/z1/Current/z1.pdf (accessed April 28, 2010)

recession set in. The inflationary aspects of this policy response, coupled with the incentives for inflation to service existing debt, would have induced a significant depreciation in the dollar (precisely the kind of significant currency depreciation that does not readily happen in the "fixed" Euro's initial response to Greece). The surplus nations who had previously converted their export-acquired dollars into dollar-denominated assets would now flee what had once been the world's "safety currency." Converting dollars into their domestic currencies and liquidating existing reserves would lead to significant appreciations in their trade-weighted value, further challenging an already diminished national export sector. All the while, banking systems around the world would fail as global credit contraction eradicated the equity positions of overleveraged institutions. As U.S. trade competiveness decreased, its current account balance would have reversed and declining imports and rising exports would begin the slow and painful restoration of world balances.

I paint this doomsday scenario in detail, during the juncture of the last U.S. recession, only because it portrays the economic calamity we delayed. The brief recession that followed only minimally impacted the U.S. and global economy. Unfortunately, it substantially increased the magnitude of the inevitable scenario to come. The vitality of the world on the dollar standard was heavily dependent on asset bubbles and the ability of the United States to go further into debt. Over the past decade, in both of these regards, the U.S. economy managed to deliver spectacularly. Throughout the real estate bubble, credit was able to expand rapidly because foreign inflows continued to enter the money supply and were multiplied across the banking system. Of course, none of this inflow would have been necessary if the United States had not steadfastly clung to its current account deficit. In 2006, the current account deficit peaked at $803 billion, around 6% of GDP.[65] The following graph depicts the surge in the current account deficit that is accompanied by an increase in the financial account surplus. As the real estate bubble began contracting in 2007, the current account began a gradual reversal but remained steadfastly in deficit.

---

65 Bureau of Economic Analysis, "U.S. International Transactions Accounts Data"

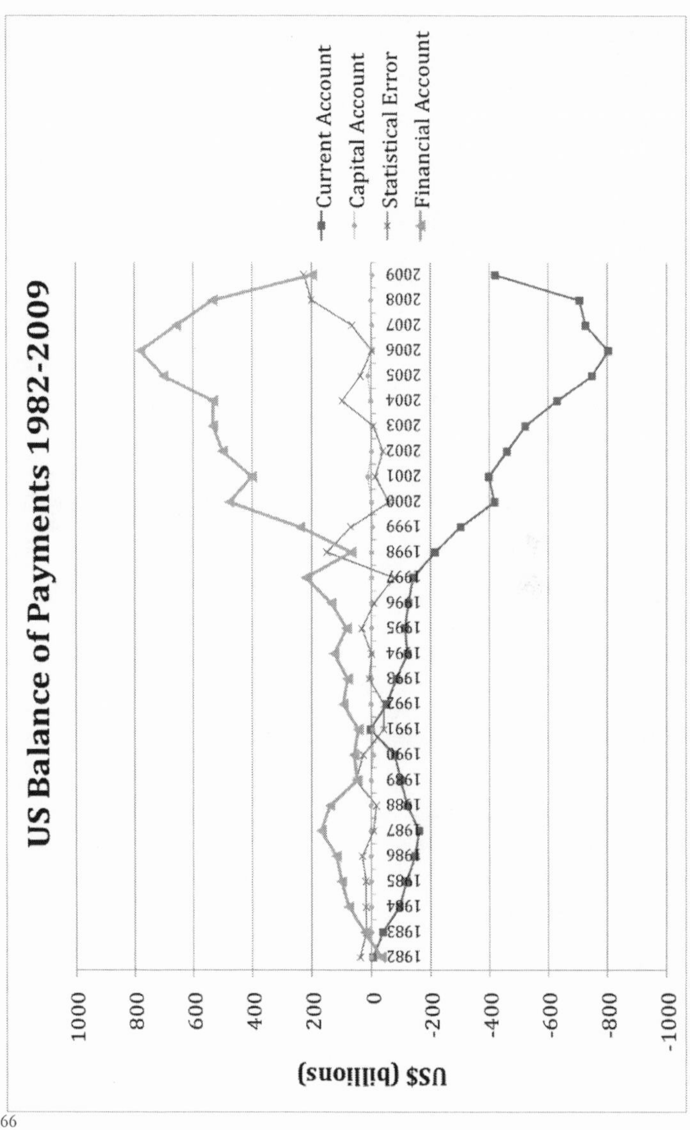

[66]

[66] Bureau of Economic Analysis, "U.S. International Transactions

This deficit in the current account was particularly tempting because the paper-backed currency was and still is the world's default reserve. Instead of reversing course, the U.S. economy was able to further ramp up its debt obligations. By 2007, at the peak of the housing bubble, credit market debt outstanding stood at $50.05 trillion, now around 3.6x GDP.[67] A significant driver of this accumulation was federal government debt more than doubling from $5.77 trillion in 2001 to $14.45 trillion in 2010.[68] President Obama's 2009 deficit alone was projected by the CBO at over $1.8 trillion.[69] From 2010-2019 the President's budget and ambitious healthcare agenda is expected to add an additional $9.27 trillion to existing government debt (uncompounded).[70] The United States has been strained and credit has become so

---

Accounts Data"

67 Federal Reserve, "Flow of Funds: Credit Market Debt Outstanding"

68 Congressional Budget Office, "A Preliminary Analysis of the President's Budget, and an Update of the CBO's Economic Outlook" http://www.cbo.gov/ftpdocs/100xx/doc10014/03-20-PresidentBudget.pdf (accessed April 28, 2010)

69 Congressional Budget Office, "A Preliminary Analysis of the President's Budget, and an Update of the CBO's Economic Outlook"

70 Congressional Budget Office, "A Preliminary Analysis of the President's Budget, and an Update of the CBO's Economic Outlook"

overextended, that the nation will soon be unable to service and increase its indebtedness to the rest of the world. But before we get ahead of ourselves in comprehending the insurmountable future burdens of United States debt, let us first delve into the particulars of the credit expansion that sustained the dollar standard over the last decade.

# Delaying the Inevitable

In my view, it was a combination of three main factors that supported the continued debt accumulation of the United States, and by extension, the export-driven growth in surplus nations: financial innovation, poor government action, and excessively loose monetary policy. At the start of the last recession, the American companies and consumers had already reached the frontier of credit expansion. Personal savings had already completed a long decline to around 2% in 2001.[71] Yet, the boom in real estate was only just beginning. The real estate bubble has been written about ad nauseam elsewhere so I will confine my discussion only as it directly relates to the current account deficit and rising debt burden. Financial innovation enabled the "diversification of risk" through a series of complex derivatives and the phenomena of

[71] Federal Reserve Bank of St. Louis (2007), "The Decline in the US Personal Savings Rate: Is It Real and Is It a Puzzle?" http://research.stlouisfed.org/publications/review/07/11/Guidolin.pdf (accessed April 28, 2010)

securitization encouraged widespread mortgage origination and leverage in the American housing market. Discussions on the workability of the Taylor rule aside, the Federal Reserve failed to identify an asset bubble and kept rates low for an extended period of time, further encouraging the expansion of debt. As housing prices rose, consumers continued to leverage home equity to fuel ever increasing consumption. Spectacularly, personal savings would turn negative by mid-2005. The corporate sector took advantage of the easy credit environment as well. At its peak in 2006, the rest of the world acquired U.S. financial assets in the form of corporate debt to the tune of $541 billion. In the third quarter of 2009, net national savings, the sum of personal, corporate, and government savings, had reached -2.5%.[72] Simultaneously, an important fundamental shift was occurring in the composition of U.S. government securities that the rest of the world was acquiring with its surpluses. Increasingly, the debt of government agencies and GSE's, such as Fannie Mae and Freddie Mac, became a prominent source of financing the current account deficit. In 2006 and

---

[72] Mandel, John (Jan 2010), "National Savings at Lowest Level Since Depression", *Innovation and Growth*, http://innovationandgrowth.wordpress.com/2010/01/04/national-savings-at-the-lowest-level-since-the-depression/ (accessed April 28, 2010)

2007, more than half of the debt acquired by foreigners came in the form of agency and GSE debt.[73]

**U.S. Government Securities Acquired by Rest of World 2005-2009[74]**

| Type | 2005 | 2006 | 2007 | 2008 | 2009 |
|---|---|---|---|---|---|
| Treasury Securities | 245.1 | 150.3 | 165.2 | 674.3 | 502.6 |
| Agency/GSE Debt | 134.3 | 222.7 | 250.3 | -218.1 | -130.1 |
| Total Gov't Securities | 379.4 | 373 | 415.5 | 456.2 | 372.5 |

Financial Assets of Note:

| | | | | | |
|---|---|---|---|---|---|
| Corporate Bonds | 328.5 | 541 | 424.6 | 40 | -99.9 |
| U.S. Equities | 56.9 | 96.2 | 218.5 | 91.2 | 122.8 |

US$ (Billions)

These numbers and shifts in financing are especially startling when considered as a fraction of the current account. The outstanding debt held by foreigners in agency and GSE securities was $1.58 trillion versus a total outstanding interest in treasury

---

73 Federal Reserve, "Flow of Funds Accounts" http://www.federalreserve.gov/releases/z1/Current/z1r-3.pdf (accessed April 28, 2010)

74 Federal Reserve, "Flow of Funds Accounts"

securities of just $2.38 trillion.[75] Since then, foreign holdings of Agency/GSE related debt have declined substantially and the line of credit extended to the United States has increasingly come in the form of treasury securities. As of the fourth quarter of 2009, outstanding foreign debt in the form of treasury securities has increased to $3.71 trillion while the Agency/GSE share has fallen to $1.32 trillion.[76] The annual transition in foreign capital inflow can be seen in the previous chart. The shift towards treasury securities is highly significant and reflects the enormous increases in government spending that have accompanied the response to the distress that began in 2007. In fact, the $1.33 trillion increase of foreign inflows into U.S. treasury securities from 2007 to 2009 is more than 54% of the entire expansion of outstanding U.S. credit market debt over the same interval.[77]

The main concern for the world going forward is whether the United States can continue to provide surplus countries with sufficient instruments for dollar-denominated investment. In other words, has the U.S. reached a limit on debt? The ability to sustain a current

---

[75] Federal Reserve, "Flow of Funds Accounts"
[76] Federal Reserve, "Flow of Funds Accounts"
[77] Federal Reserve, "Flow of Funds Accounts"

account deficit will be instrumental in keeping the engine functioning and the train of the global economy on its track. It is not surprising that we see a strong correlation between the current account balance and the growth of the economy. Equity markets have strongly reflected this over the past 30 years. As the current account deficit first began expanding in earnest around 1982, equity markets skyrocketed and the Dow Jones Industrial Average doubled over the next 5 years. In 1987, the Dow suffered its infamous Black Monday crash on October 19 with the Dow plunging 508 points, around a quarter of its value in a single day.[78]

Interestingly, starting in 1987 the current account had also begun to trend back in the direction of surplus. Indeed, a surplus was achieved in 1991, which not surprisingly coincides with the recession of the early 90s. From 1991 to 2006, the size of the annual current account deficit grew every single year with only one exception- 2001. The Dow rose from 3,204 to 12,526 as the current account balance swung from a $2.8 billion surplus to an $803 billion deficit. The one modest contraction in the deficit, 2001, was marked by a brief recession and equity depreciation.

---

[78] CNBC (Oct 2007), "Remembering the Crash of '87" http://www.cnbc.com/id/20910471/ (accessed April 29, 2010)

From 2006-2009, the deficit began trending back towards surplus once more and was nearly halved falling to just $420 billion by 2009. Equity prices depreciated substantially over this interval as well. The following chart depicts the performance of the Dow Jones Industrial Average and the size of the current account deficit. A simple regression finds that the correlation between the two is statistically significant with a 95% confidence interval and that 77% of the variation in the value of the Dow can be explained by fluctuations in the current account deficit.[79] Although the limits of economic forecasting do not enable this relationship to "predict" the daily movements of the Dow, it establishes a strong inverse correlation between equity markets and the current account over the past several decades. If expectations for a correction of imbalance set in and the current account trends back towards surplus, we can expect a parallel depreciation in U.S. equity markets.

---

[79] STATA, "Regression Analysis" conducted on Harvard University servers on April 29, 2009

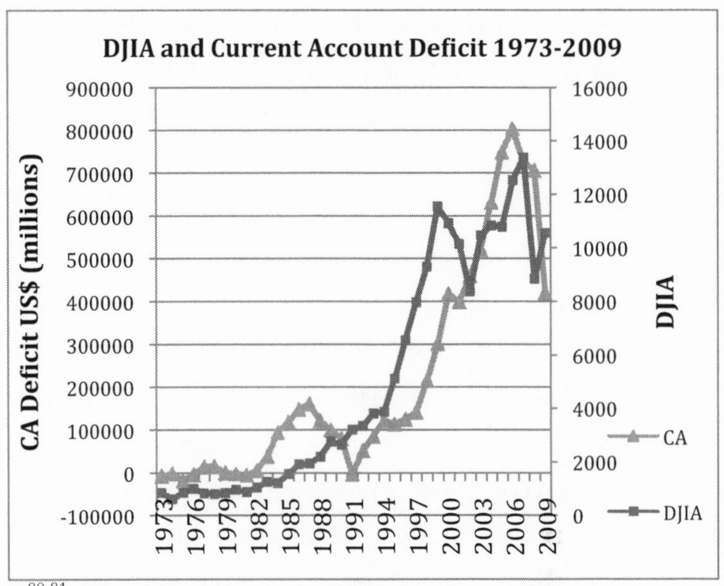


[80] [81] *All unaccounted statistics from preceding paragraph cite this data as well.

The widening current account deficit provided the world with large dollar surpluses that they were able to invest in U.S. assets to finance a credit expansion. However, the United States is reaching the point where credit has been extended beyond capacity for repayment. Consumers have become accustomed to living beyond their means and have become

---

[80] Dow Jones Indexes, "Index Price History" http://www.djaverages.com/?view=industrial&page=reports&show=performance&symbol=DJI (accessed April 29, 2010)
[81] Bureau of Economic Analysis, "U.S. International Transactions Accounts Data"

increasingly strained. In 2009, consumer credit contracted by $113 billion to $2.4 trillion.[82] It was the first contraction in consumer credit in more than 53 years since data recording began in 1956.[83] The accumulation of corporate debt has also slowed as seen in the next chart, and total business debt actually experienced a slight contraction to $10.9 trillion in 2009.[84] Most significantly, the engine of the U.S. consumption over the past decade, the expansion of housing market credit, has finally begun to reverse course. The consumption fueled by the housing boom not only sustained the U.S. economy, but also the global economy. Yet, when credit finally contracts and new loan issuances and mortgage originations become unable to finance existing obligations, tremendous pain will be inflicted in the form of a collapse in the U.S. and abroad. The first stage of this global contraction was the financial crisis. The losses in the financial

---

[82] Federal Reserve Board, "D1 Seasonally Adjusted Debt Growth by Sector (Quarterly)" http://www.federalreserve.gov/datadownload/Download.aspx?rel=Z1&series=c2ddb43afa6e2d083658b59f296e8f87&lastObs=25&from=&to=&filetype=csv&label=include&layout=seriesrow&type=package (accessed April 29, 2010)

[83] Federal Reserve, "1996 Flow of Funds Accounts" http://www.federalreserve.gov/releases/z1/19960912/z1.pdf (accessed April 29, 2010)

[84] Federal Reserve Board, "D1 Seasonally Adjusted Debt Growth by Sector (Quarterly)"

sector were inevitable because it was so heavily dependent on leverage and the expansion of credit for growth. For now, only the massive and unsustainable increases in U.S. federal government spending are keeping the world economy afloat.

| **% Growth by Year**[85] | Home Mortgage Credit | Consumer Credit | Corporate Debt | Federal Gov't Debt |
|---|---|---|---|---|
| 2000 | 8.7 | 11.4 | 8.5 | -8 |
| 2001 | 10.6 | 8.6 | 4.5 | -0.2 |
| 2002 | 13.3 | 5.6 | 0.7 | 7.6 |
| 2003 | 14.6 | 5.3 | 1.8 | 10.9 |
| 2004 | 13.4 | 5.6 | 4.1 | 9 |
| 2005 | 13.2 | 4.5 | 6.5 | 7 |
| 2006 | 11 | 4.1 | 8.5 | 3.9 |
| 2007 | 6.7 | 5.8 | 13.1 | 4.9 |
| 2008 | -0.6 | 1.5 | 5.1 | 24.2 |
| 2009 | -1.6 | -4.3 | 1.4 | 22.7 |

[85] Federal Reserve Board, "D1 Seasonally Adjusted Debt Growth by Sector (Annual)" http://www.federalreserve.gov/datadownload/Download.aspx?rel=Z1&series=10ff9fec77b23c0f7eef5cb162912116&lastObs=25&from=&to=&filetype=csv&label=include&layout=seriesrow&type=package (accessed April 29, 2010)

Observe the surge in growth of the federal debt that began in 2008. Moreover, the actual debt burden of the United States government is growing at a rate even more alarming than published figures as a result of convenient accounting practices. In Charles Goyette's *The Dollar Meltdown*, it is estimated that even if the budget were balanced, unfunded liabilities, such as Social Security and Medicare, would continue to grow at over $2 trillion a year.[86] Since programs such as Social Security were receiving more than they paid out from 1998-2001, the government's budget recorded a surplus even though the costs of underlying demographic shifts far outpaced this supposed "savings."[87] Revenues soared as a result of the bubble in technology, leading to promises of future tax cuts. After the bubble popped, those tax cuts were still enacted, increasing the debt of the government even further and moving it permanently into deficit since 2001. The ability of the U.S. government to raise debt is currently the only support preventing global economic crisis. In 2010, the U.S. federal debt stands

---

[86] Goyette, Charles, *The Dollar Meltdown,* P. 39 (Penguin Group 2009)

[87] Duncan, Richard, *The Dollar Crisis,* (Wiley 2003)

at 94.27% of GDP.[88] As with severely indebted countries around the world, such as Greece or Japan, nobody can be sure just how high the U.S. federal debt can rise before credit contraction sets in or faith is lost in its currency. Despite massive spending, indicators have already begun to emerge that the federal deficits may not be large enough to combat a global crisis via Keynesianism. Outstanding total credit market debt has been contracting since the second quarter of 2009, and has marked the first instance of year-over-year declines in total United States debt in the post-World War II era.[89]

---

[88] USGovernmentSpending.com, "US Federal Debt as a Percentage of GDP" http://www.usgovernmentspending.com/federal_debt_chart.html (accessed April 30, 2010)

[89] Federal Reserve Board, "L1 Credit Market Debt Outstanding (Quarterly)"

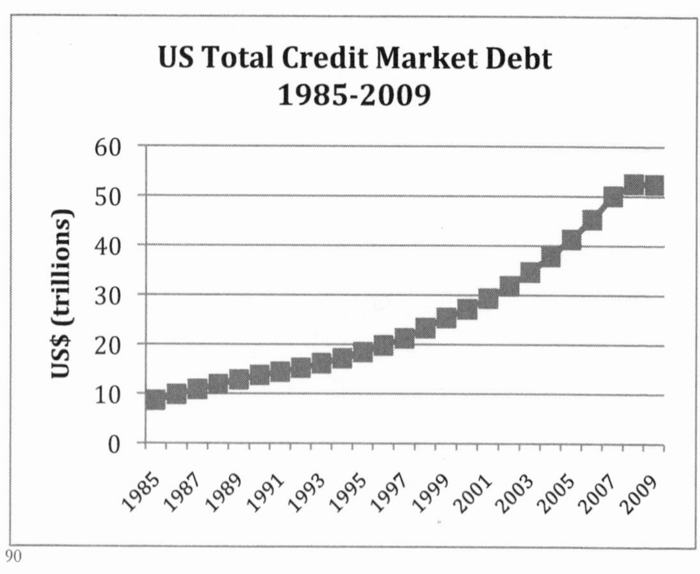


90

Ironically, interest expense for the United States is far outpacing GDP growth and fiscal and monetary actions promise to increase the money supply. Yet, interest rates across the maturity spectrum have recently remained extraordinary low. Unless credit contracts rapidly over the next few years and strong deflationary pressures set in, there is simply no reason why the United States should continue to be able to

---

[90] Federal Reserve Board, "L1 Credit Market Debt Outstanding (Annual)" http://www.federalreserve.gov/datadownload/Download.aspx?rel=Z1&series=db1e9b17d96d117b205c178203db13b9&lastObs=25&from=&to=&filetype=csv&label=include&layout=seriesrow&type=package (accessed April 30, 2010)

borrow at such attractive rates. Indeed, the arrangement hardly seems to be rational and Treasury CDS have spiked and are now pricing in around a 5% chance of default over the next 5 years.[91] Nonetheless, more likely than not, the U.S. government spending will be able to reverse the first contraction that has occurred in total credit market debt over the past few quarters. Foreign exporters seem more than willing to finance exceedingly large deficits.

---

[91] Reuters (Feb 2010), "Treasury CDS off Highs as Worries Persist"
http://www.reuters.com/article/idUSN0524400220100205
(accessed April 30, 2010)

# Dollar Decline: Correcting the Drivers of Imbalance

As Richard Duncan highlights in *The Dollar Crisis,* one of the main reasons the United States runs such a large trade deficit is that low-cost labor in the rest of the world is fundamentally more well suited to produce goods at a lower cost than domestic manufacturers can.[92] At the most basic level, Americans buy foreign goods because they are cheaper, not because the rest of the world so readily finances us. As long as the dollar maintains its current purchasing power, low-cost labor will remain abroad, current account deficits of the United States will continue, foreign exporters will invest in dollar-denominated assets, asset bubbles will persist, and the ultimate correction of imbalances will escalate in severity. Simultaneously, the combination of a slowing economy along with increased expenditures to maintain credit,

---

92 Duncan, Richard, *The Dollar Crisis,* (Wiley 2003)

the current account deficit, rising social welfare costs, and the servicing of existing debt have accelerated the path of government spending. The current trajectory is not perpetually sustainable and when the United States finally experiences fiscal, the result will be much more painful than its financial precursor.

The only way to rectify the imbalances is through a correction in the appetite of Americans for foreign goods. At the present, the wage difference between the United States and surplus nations is devastatingly large and the dollar remains extraordinarily overvalued. The last major depreciation the dollar experienced was from 1985 to 1988 when it lost half of its value. In those three years, the dollar index plummeted from 160 in 1985 to around 85 at the start of 1988.[93] The current account deficit, which had hovered around 3% of GDP for several years, peaked at $160 billion in 1987 and soon followed the trend set by the dollar, correcting to a surplus by 1991.[94] The dollar index continued its slide to around 80 by 1991.[95]

---

93 ShareLynx Gold, "DX – US Dollar Index Charting Data" http://www.chartsrus.com/chart.php?image=http://www.sharelynx.com/chartstemp/free/chartind1CRUvoi.php?ticker=FUTDX (accessed May 1, 2010)

94 Bureau of Economic Analysis, "U.S. International Transactions Accounts Data"

95 ShareLynx Gold, "DX – US Dollar Index Charting Data"

Much of the recent evidence seems to suggest that the next major decline of the dollar has already begun. The imbalance this time, however, is much more severe. The current account deficit most recently peaked at $803 billion in 2006, around 6% of GDP.[96] Yet, the dollar has only fallen around 30% from its last local peak in 2002.[97]

Part of the reason the dollar has remained so strong, despite continued current account deficits is that markets have yet to impose any sort of panic on its floating exchange rates. To the contrary, the dollar has served as a haven during the recent global economic turmoil. Having an overvalued currency dampens the U.S. export sector (much like the strong Euro now impacts Greece) and encourages continued imbalance. This apparent inefficiency in pricing stems from the policy positions of central bankers around the world. In particular, surplus nations with fixed exchange rates, such as China, have exacerbated the overvaluation of the dollar by accumulating large amounts of foreign dollar assets and preventing the Yuan from appreciating. The success of this policy in encouraging export-driven growth is largely visible in the

---

96 Bureau of Economic Analysis, "U.S. International Transactions Accounts Data"

97 ShareLynx Gold, "DX – US Dollar Index Charting Data"

progression of the trade balance of China and the United States. As household consumption falls in the U.S., the appetite for Chinese goods will diminish, a shift that has already been reflected in the most recent current account data.

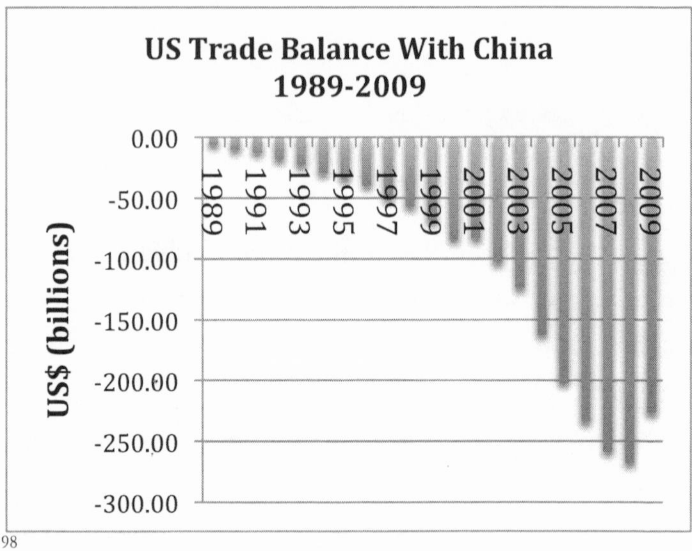


[98]

More importantly, a decline in the trade-weighted value of the dollar will further harm the Chinese export sector. The Chinese government and central bank must negotiate a perilous path in their

---

[98] US Census Bureau, "Trade in Goods with China" http://www.census.gov/foreign-trade/balance/c5700.html#2010 (accessed May 1, 2010)

decision to allow for Yuan appreciation. In doing so, they risk not only dampening their export sector, but also substantially reducing the value of their existing dollar assets. Any abrupt action by the central bank to lessen its exposure to declines by selling dollar denominated assets would also inspire significant herd behavior by other nations with dollar stakes. The European Union, running a trade surplus of over $60.5 billion with the U.S. in 2009, finds itself in a similar imbalance.[99] However, unlike China, it does not enjoy the luxury of a booming economy. The widespread structural deficiencies in the Eurozone and challenges of maintaining a shared currency will prevent it from assuming the deficits necessary to sustain global growth as the U.S. current account corrects itself. Without any remaining engine to support demand and world credit expansion, the global economy will face an increasingly severe downturn. As Harvard Professor Martin Feldstein has noted, Europe will be plagued by rising unemployment and the fall in demand for their

---

[99] US Census Bureau, "Trade in Goods with European Union" http://www.census.gov/foreign-trade/balance/c0003.html (accessed May 1, 2010)

products "will cause a slowdown in Europe's already weak growth."[100]

There is also reason to believe that the ultimate fall in the dollar value will be particularly acute. The downward movement in the currency will likely not be mere readjustment, but rather absolute collapse. The longer the current imbalances are sustained, the more likely a hyperinflation scenario becomes. We have already discussed the declining fiscal condition of the United States at length. In the current environment, the economic slowdown has introduced deflationary pressures that have strengthened the resolve of policymakers to respond with stimulus and face little risk of inflation. Deflationary concerns are absolutely unfounded. As Brandon Adams notes in *The Setting Sun*: "If the Federal Reserve has a desire to create inflation, they will succeed."[101] In 2002 speech to the National Economists Club, then Federal Reserve Governor Ben Bernanke stated, "Under a paper-money system, a determined government can always generate

---

[100] National Bureau of Economic Research, *Martin Feldstein-Financial Times* (Aug 2006), "Europe has to face threat of America's trade deficit" http://www.nber.org/feldstein/ft080206.pdf (accessed May 1, 2010)

[101] Adams 19

higher spending and hence positive inflation."[102] The unprecedented size of the fiscal response, unorthodox lending programs, and direct intervention into securities markets by the Federal Reserve and Treasury have introduced tremendous liquidity into the system. Ultimately, this liquidity may prove difficult to withdraw especially if global imbalances necessitate continued pressure towards credit creation. If the creditworthiness of the United States government declines, inflationary expectations will undoubtedly surge alongside the costs of financing. Tremendous inflation, or even hyperinflation, will drive down the value of the dollar by far more than appreciation in prices, eventually rectifying the conditions that enabled prolonged current account deficits.

---

[102] Federal Reserve Board, *Remarks by Governor Ben S. Bernanke* (Nov 2002), "Deflation: Making Sure "It" Doesn't Happen Here" http://www.federalreserve.gov/boardDocs/speeches/2002/20021121/default.htm (accessed May 1, 2010)

# Looking to the Future

The prospects for avoiding the inevitable decline of the dollar are slim. Fundamentally, the only effective solution would be to establish a reserve currency that forbids sustained imbalances, excessive credit creation, and asset bubbles. Despite some of gold's inherent automatic stabilizing mechanisms, our discussion and the historical verdict has largely repudiated a commodity-backed currency. The system would necessarily have to fine countries that deviated from balances in the current account in order to ensure a prompt return to equilibrium.

We need only look as far the current crisis in the Eurozone to know that such a system is unfeasible. The enforcement mechanisms in the European Monetary Union have proven unworkable because they would exacerbate conditions for deficit countries such as Greece and Portugal who are already facing horrendous economic realities. Moreover, without countercyclical policy to run deficits during downturns, more instability is also created. Naturally, an "impartial" organization such as the IMF might be able to operate within a reinvented monetary system in order to prevent contractions in money supply and mitigate defaults on foreign debt obligations. Yet, the history of the IMF also proves that intervention creates a new source of significant distress. Namely, the moral hazard introduced by any sort of last-resort backstop within a stable international monetary framework, would make a global reserve currency spectacularly unsustainable. Just as the Eurozone struggles to obtain an optimal currency area because of political divergence and cultural barriers to labor mobility, a global economy under an "impartial" world reserve currency would suffer the same challenges. Indeed, given the friction that perpetually exists among nation states and the extraordinary imbalances between the developing and developed world, any sort of globally objective system is destined for failure. For the time being, the dollar will, in all likelihood, continue to be the overvalued currency of choice.

Although I won't pretend to have a solution to the economic problems of sovereign leverage, be they in the imminent crisis of the Eurozone or the future crisis of global imbalance, there are a few suggestions I would like to make in closing. The developing world must continue to ambulate on the path of economic empowerment. However, surplus nations such as China must transition towards domestic-driven economic expansion while gradually diminishing their dependence on exports. Rising wages and appreciating currencies must be viewed not with disdain, but rather as an opportunity to instill the foundations of markets for new sources of domestic demand. I also feel very strongly about the benefits of free trade. While it is true that the liberalization of trade has enabled the creation of substantial trade imbalances, it has also undeniably delivered prosperity by comparative advantage across the globe. The economic structure of the Eurozone encourages trade but is also plagued by labor immobility. The world under free trade faces this challenge to an exponentially greater extent. More labor mobility can come about as a result of shifts in immigration laws, but political, cultural, and fiscal concerns clearly make any change impracticable.

The point is that we can't abandon the forces that sustain global imbalances. Ultimately, perception is reality and if the world can agree to continue buying dollar-denominated assets, the United States will continue to purchase the exports of the world. The opinions put forth here are hardly those of a modern Cassandra. While the correction of global imbalances may be inevitable, the world may also continue to develop ingenious methods of credit expansion that will continue to sustain massive deficits. To be certain, the global economy can remain overheated, and its currencies mispriced, far longer than a speculative investor might remain solvent. A global crisis is certainly "imminent," but the precise timetable for the reversal of imbalances, whether measured in days or decades, remains the trillion-dollar question.

# Bibliography

Adams, Brandon, *The Setting Sun: The End of US Economic Dominance* (Publishing Pending 2010).

Bloomberg, "Greek Bonds Slide as Debt Concerns Pushes Up Premium Over Bunds" http://www.bloomberg.com/apps/news?pid=20601009&sid=avNkHG1eWlF4 (accessed March 4, 2010).

Breuss, Fritz, *The stability and growth pact: experience and future aspects* (Springer 2007).

Burak Gundagdu and Orkun Girban (2006), "Greece's Integration to the EMU and Lessons for Turkey", *Turkish Central Bank*, http://www.tcmb.gov.tr/yeni/iletisimgm/B_Gundogdu-O_Girban.pdf (accessed March 1, 2010).

Bureau of Economic Analysis, "U.S. International Transactions Accounts Data" http://www.bea.gov/international/bp_web/list.cfm?anon=71®istered=0 (accessed April 28, 2010).

CIA World Factbook, "Germany" https://www.cia.gov/library/publications/the-world-factbook/geos/gm.html (accesses March 4, 2010).

CIA Worldfactbook, "Germany and France" https://www.cia.gov/library/publications/the-world-factbook/geos.html (accessed March 4, 2010).

CNBC (October 2007), "Remembering the Crash of '87" http://www.cnbc.com/id/20910471/ (accessed April 29, 2010).

CNBC (April 2010), "Greece Just Tip of Debt Crisis Iceberg: Roubini" http://classic.cnbc.com/id/36795861/ (accessed April 27, 2010).

Cohan, William, *House of Cards: A Tale of Hubris and Wretched Excess on Wall Street* (Doubleday 2009).

Congressional Budget Office, "A Preliminary Analysis of the President's Budget, and an Update of the CBO's Economic Outlook" http://www.cbo.gov/ftpdocs/100xx/doc10014/03-20-PresidentBudget.pdf (accessed April 28, 2010).

Dalton, Mathew (February 2010), "EU Statistics Agency: Greek Debt Will Rise Due to 2001 Swap", *The Wall Street Journal*, http://online.wsj.com/article/BT-CO-20100224-712984.html (accessed March 3, 2010).

Daniel Yergin and Joseph Stanislaw (1997), "Commanding Heights: Nixon Tries Price Controls", *PBS*, http://www.pbs.org/wgbh/commandingheights/shared/minitextlo/ess nixongold.html (accessed April 26, 2010).

Dow Jones Indexes, "Index Price History" http://www.djaverages.com/?view=industrial&page=reports&show=performance&symbol=DJI (accessed April 29, 2010).

Duncan, Richard, *The Dollar Crisis: Causes, Consequences, Cures* (Wiley 2003).

European Commission (2010), "Report on Greek Government Deficit and Debt Statistics" http://epp.eurostat.ec.europa.eu/cache/ITY P UBLIC/COM 2010 REPORT GREEK/EN/COM 2010 REPORT GREEK-EN.PDF (accessed March 3, 2010).

European Commission Eurostat, "Excesive Debt Procedures" http://epp.eurostat.ec.europa.eu/portal/page/portal/government finance statistics/excessive deficit (accessed March 1, 2010).

European Commission Eurostat, http://epp.eurostat.ec.europa.eu/portal/page/portal/eurostat/home/ (accessed March 2, 2010).

Federal Reserve, "1996 Flow of Funds Accounts" http://www.federalreserve.gov/releases/z1/19960912/z1.pdf (accessed April 29, 2010).

Federal Reserve, "Flow of Funds: Credit Market Debt Outstanding" http://www.federalreserve.gov/releases/z1/Current/z1.pdf (accessed April 28, 2010).

Federal Reserve, "Flow of Funds Accounts" http://www.federalreserve.gov/releases/z1/Current/z1r-3.pdf (accessed April 28, 2010).

Federal Reserve Bank of St. Louis (2007), "The Decline in the US Personal Savings Rate: Is It Real and Is It a Puzzle?" http://research.stlouisfed.org/publications/review/07/11/Guidolin.pdf (accessed April 28, 2010).

Federal Reserve Board, "D1 Seasonally Adjusted Debt Growth by Sector (Annual)" http://www.federalreserve.gov/datadownload/Download.aspx?rel=Z1&series=10ff9fec77b23c0f7eef5cb162912116&lastObs=25&from=&to=&filetype=csv&label=include&layout=seriesrow&type=package (accessed April 29, 2010).

Federal Reserve Board, "D1 Seasonally Adjusted Debt Growth by Sector (Quarterly)" http://www.federalreserve.gov/datadownload/Download.aspx?rel=Z1&series=c2ddb43afa6e2d083658b59f296e8f87&lastObs=25&from=&to=

&filetype=csv&label=include&layout=seriesrow &type=package (accessed April 29, 2010).

Federal Reserve Board, "L1 Credit Market Debt Outstanding (Annual)" http://www.federalreserve.gov/datadownload/Download.aspx?rel=Z1&series=db1e9b17d96d117b205c178203db13b9&lastObs=25&from=&to=&filetype=csv&label=include&layout=seriesrow&type=package (accessed April 30, 2010).

Frankel, Jeffrey (1997), "The Endogeneity of the Optimum Currency Area Criteria", *The University of California, Berkeley*, http://faculty.haas.berkeley.edu/arose/ocaej.pdf (accessed February 27, 2010).

Goyette, Charles, *The Dollar Meltdown,* (Penguin Group 2009).

Heinz, F.F (2006), "Cross Border Labour Mobility Within an Enlarged EU" http://www.ecb.int/pub/pdf/scpops/ecbocp52.pdf (accessed February 27, 2010).

International Monetary Fund, "IMF World Economic Outlook Database" http://www.imf.org/external/pubs/ft/weo/2009/01/weodata/index.aspx (accessed April 29, 2010).

International Monetary Fund, "International Monetary Statistics Trial" http://www.imfstatistics.org/imf/ (accessed April 29, 2010).

IntercontinentalExchange, "ICE U.S. Dollar Index (USDX)" https://www.theice.com/productguide/ProductGroupHierarchy.shtml?groupDetail=&group.groupId=17 (accessed April 28, 2010).

Federal Reserve Board, *Remarks by Governor Ben S. Bernanke* (November 2002), "Deflation: Making Sure "It" Doesn't Happen Here" http://www.federalreserve.gov/boardDocs/speeches/2002/20021121/default.htm (accessed May 1, 2010).

Jones, Sam (February 2010), "Hedge fund prosper from Greek debt", *Financial Times*, http://www.ft.com/cms/s/0/a6b71b50-249f-11df-8be0-00144feab49a.html (accessed March 5 2010).

Landon Thomas and Nicholas Kulish (April 2010), "I.M.F. Promises More Aid for Greece as European Crisis Grows", *The New York Times*, http://www.nytimes.com/2010/04/29/business/global/29euro.html?hp (accessed April 27, 2010).

Mandel, John (January 2010), "National Savings at Lowest Level Since Depression", *Innovation and Growth*, http://innovationandgrowth.wordpress.com/20

10/01/04/national-savings-at-the-lowest-level-since-the-depression/ (accessed April 28, 2010).

Moneyweek.com (February 2010), "Greece: Credit Rating Slash Spooks Stocks". http://www.moneyweek.com/investments/stock-markets/greece-credit-rating-cut-46503.aspx (accessed March 3, 2010).

Mundell, R.A. (1961), "A Theory of Optimum Currency Areas", *American Economic Review.*

National Bureau of Economic Research, *Martin Feldstein-Financial Times* (August 2006), "Europe has to face threat of America's trade deficit" http://www.nber.org/feldstein/ft080206.pdf (accessed May 1, 2010).

Noelwatson.com, "Lehman CDS" http://www.noelwatson.com/blog/content/binary/LehmanCDS29012009.gif (accessed March 5, 2010).

Oakley, David (February 2010), "Moody's joins S&P in warning on Greece" http://www.ft.com/cms/s/0/a88ef798-21f9-11df-98dd-00144feab49a.html (accessed March 3, 2010).

Our Campagins, "US President National Vote Race Details – Nov 07, 1972" http://www.ourcampaigns.com/RaceDetail.html?RaceID=1939 (accessed April 26, 2010).

Reuters (February 2010), "Treasury CDS off Highs as Worries Persist" http://www.reuters.com/article/idUSN0524400220100205 (accessed April 30, 2010).

ShareLynx Gold, "DX – US Dollar Index Charting Data" http://www.chartsrus.com/chart.php?image=http://www.sharelynx.com/chartstemp/free/chartind1CRUvoi.php?ticker=FUTDX (accessed May 1, 2010).

STATA, "Regression Analysis" conducted on Harvard University servers on April 29, 2009.

Stauffer, Amity, "What is the European Monetary Union", *The University of Iowa Center for International Finance and Development*, http://www.uiowa.edu/ifdebook/faq/faq_docs/EMU.shtml (accessed February 27, 2010).

The Associated Press (March 2010), "ECB Holds Rates, Withdrawing Some Crisis Measures" http://www.nytimes.com/aponline/2010/03/04/business/AP-EU-Europe-Interest-Rates.html (accessed March 4, 2010).

The Economist (February 2010), "Greece's Soverign Debt Crunch: A very European Crisis" http://www.economist.com/world/europe/displaystory.cfm?story_id=15452594 (accessed March 3, 2010).

Thomson Reuters, "Global Soverign Credit Default Swaps" http://blogs.reuters.com/rolfe-winkler/files/2010/02/kyd77h.jpg (accessed March 4, 2010).

Thomson Reuters, *The Economist (Feb 2010),* "Greece's Sovereign Debt Crunch: A very European Crisis".

United States Treasury Department, "Major Holders of Treasury Securities" http://www.treas.gov/tic/mfh.txt (accessed April 28, 2010).

US Census Bureau, "Trade in Goods with China" http://www.census.gov/foreign-trade/balance/c5700.html#2010 (accessed May 1, 2010).

US Census Bureau, "Trade in Goods with European Union" http://www.census.gov/foreign-trade/balance/c0003.html (accessed May 1, 2010).

USGovernmentSpending.com, "US Federal Debt as a Percentage of GDP" http://www.usgovernmentspending.com/federal_debt_chart.html (accessed April 30, 2010).

Wall Street Journal (April 2010), "Greek Central Banker Urges More Cuts" http://online.wsj.com/article/SB1000142405274

8704471204575209651683066756.html (accessed April 27, 2010).

Webb, Merryn (February 2010), "Why Germany should dump the Euro", *Moneyweek.com*, http://www.moneyweek.com/blog/why-germany-should-dump-the-euro-00122.aspx (accessed March 4, 2010).

World Bank, World Development Indicators, http://www.google.com/publicdata (accessed March 1, 2010).

Worldbank, "Key Development and Data Statistics" http://web.worldbank.org/WBSITE/EXTERNAL/DATASTATISTICS/0,,contentMDK:20535285~menuPK:1192694~pagePK:64133150~piPK:64133175~theSitePK:239419,00.html (accessed March 1, 2010).

XRates.com, "Euro to 1 USD" http://www.xrates.com/d/EUR/USD/graph120.html (accessed March 4, 2010).

Yahoo! Finance, "NASDAQ Composite (^IXIC) Historical Prices" http://finance.yahoo.com/q/hp?s=%5EIXIC (accessed April 28, 2010).

# About the Author

Grant Wonders is a sophomore at Harvard College where he is currently pursuing a degree in Economics and a secondary in Archaeology. "The Imminent Crisis" was inspired by his work in a Harvard Economics Department tutorial. This is his first published work.

4137336R00083

Made in the USA
San Bernardino, CA
04 September 2013